Dog Knitting Projects

Adorable and Stunning Ideas For Knit Dog

Copyright © 2023

DEDICATION

Contents

Beagle

The Beagle is a neat little dog, so make yours stand up very straight, with the tail bending over slightly.

You Will Need

- Small amount of Rowan Cashsoft Yarn 4ply in Bluebottle 449 (bb) for collar
- 10g (1?4oz) of Rowan Pure Wool 4ply in Black 404 (bl)
- 10g (1?4oz) of Rowan Pure Wool 4ply in Ochre 461 (oc)
- 15g (1?2oz) of Rowan Pure Wool 4ply in Snow 412 (sn)
- 23?4mm (US 2) Double Pointed Knitting Needles (for holding stitches)
- Pair of 23?4mm (US 2) Knitting Needles
- 3 Pipe Cleaner(s) for legs and tail

1

Step 1

Right Back Leg

With sn, cast on 11 sts.

Beg with a k row, work 2 rows st st.

Row 3: Inc, k2, k2tog, k1, k2tog, k2, inc. (11 sts)

Row 4: Purl.

Rep rows 3–4 once more.

Row 7: K2tog, k7, k2tog.* (9 sts)

Work 3 rows st st.

Row 11: K2tog, k1, inc, k1, inc, k1, k2tog. (9 sts)

Row 12: Purl.

Rep rows 11–12 once more.

Row 15: K3, inc, k1, inc, k3. (11 sts)

Row 16: Purl.**

Join in oc.

Row 17: K4sn, incsn, k1sn, incsn, k2sn, k2oc. (13 sts)

Row 18: P2oc, p11sn.

Row 19: K5sn, incsn,

k3oc. (15 sts)

Row 20: P3oc, p12sn.

Row 21: K6sn, incsn,

k3oc. (17 sts)

Row 22: P4oc, p13sn.

Row 23: K7sn, incsn,

k4oc. (19 sts)

Row 24: P4oc, p15sn.

Row 25: Cast (bind) off 9 sts sn, k6sn icos, k4oc (hold 10 sts on spare needle for Right Side of Body).

Step 2

Left Back Leg

Work as for Right Back Leg to **.

Join in oc.

Row 17: K2oc, k2sn, incsn, k1sn, incsn, k4sn. (13 sts)

Row 18: P11sn, p2oc.

Row 19: K3oc, k2sn, incsn, k1sn, incsn, k5sn. (15 sts)

Row 20: P12sn, p3oc.

Row 21: K3oc, k3sn, incsn, k1sn, incsn, k6sn. (17 sts)

Row 22: P13sn, p4oc.

Row 23: K4oc, k3sn, incsn, k1sn, incsn, k7sn. (19 sts)

Row 24: P15sn, p4oc.

Row 25: K4oc, k6sn, cast (bind) off 9 sts sn (hold 10 sts on spare needle for Left Side

of Body).

Step 3

Right Front Leg

Work as for Right Back Leg to *.

Work 7 rows st st.

Join in oc.

Row 15: Incsn, k4sn, k2oc, k1sn, incsn. (11 sts)

Row 16: P1sn, p4oc, p6sn.

Row 17: Incsn, k4sn, k5oc, incoc. (13 sts) Row 18: P7oc, p6sn.

Row 19: Cast (bind) off 6 sts sn, k7oc icos (hold 7 sts on spare needle for Right Side of Body).

Step 4

Left Front Leg

Work as for Right Back Leg to *.

Work 7 rows st st.

Join in oc.

Row 15: Incsn, k1sn, k2oc, k4sn, incsn. (11 sts)

Row 16: P6sn, p4oc, p1sn.

Row 17: Incsn, k5oc, k4sn, incsn. (13 sts) Row 18: P6sn, p7oc.

Row 19: K7oc, cast (bind) off 6 sts sn (hold 7 sts on spare needle for Left Side of Body).

Step 5

Right Side of Body

Row 1: With oc and bl, cast on 1 st oc, with RS facing k7oc from spare needle of Right Front Leg, cast on 1 st oc and 5 sts bl. (14 sts) Row 2: P5bl, p9oc.

Row 3: K9oc, k5bl, cast on 6 sts bl. (20 sts) Row 4: P11bl, p9oc.

Join in sn.

Row 5: Incoc, k9oc, k10bl, cast on 2 sts bl and 2 sts oc, with RS facing k2oc, k3sn, k5oc from spare needle of Right Back Leg, cast on 1 st oc. (36 sts)

Row 6: P7oc, p2sn, p3oc, p13bl, p11oc. Row 7: K11oc, k13bl, k3oc, k1sn, k8oc. Row 8: P11oc, p14bl, p11oc.

Row 9: K11oc, k16bl, k9oc.

Row 10: P9oc, p15bl, p12oc.

Row 11: Incoc, k11oc, k16bl, k8oc. (37 sts) Row 12: P7oc, p17bl, p12oc, p1sn.

Row 13: K1sn, k11oc, k19bl, k6oc.

Row 14: P5oc, p20bl, p10oc, p2sn.

Row 15: K2sn, k9oc, k23bl, k3oc.

Row 16: P2oc, p24bl, p6oc, p2bl, p3sn. Row 17: K3sn, k3bl, k4oc, k27bl.

Row 18: P2togbl, p26bl, p2oc, p5bl, p2sn. (36 sts)

Row 19: K1sn, k33bl, k2togbl. (35 sts) Row 20: P5bl (hold 5 sts on spare needle for tail), cast (bind) off 19 sts bl, p10bl icos, p1sn (hold 11 sts on spare needle for

right neck).

Step 6

Left Side of Body

Row1: Withocandbl,caston1stoc,with WS facing p7oc from spare needle of Left Front Leg, cast on 1 st oc and 5 sts bl. (14 sts) Row 2: K5bl, k9oc.

Row 3: P9oc, p5bl, cast on 6 sts bl. (20 sts) Row 4: K11bl, k9oc.

Join in sn.

Row 5: Incoc, p9oc, p10bl, cast on 2 sts bl and 2 sts oc, with WS facing p2oc, p3sn, p5oc from spare needle of Left Back Leg, cast on 1 st oc. (36 sts)

Row 6: K7oc, k2sn, k3oc, k13bl, k11oc. Row 7: P11oc, p13bl, p3oc, p1sn, p8oc. Row 8: K11oc, k14bl, k11oc.

Row 9: P11oc, p16bl, p9oc.

Row 10: K9oc, k15bl, k12oc.

Row 11: Incoc, p11oc, p16bl, p8oc. (37 sts) Row 12: K7oc, k17bl, k12oc, k1sn.

Row 13: P1sn, p11oc, p19bl, p6oc.

Row 14: K5oc, k20bl, k10oc, k2sn.

Row 15: P2sn, p9oc, p23bl, p3oc.

Row 16: K2oc, k24bl, k6oc, k2bl, k3sn. Row 17: P3sn, p3bl, p4oc, p27bl.

Row 18: K2togbl, k26bl, k2oc, k5bl, k2sn. (36 sts)

Row 19: P1sn, p33bl, p2togbl. (35 sts) Row 20: K5bl (hold 5 sts on spare needle for tail), cast (bind) off 19 sts bl, k10bl icos, k1sn (hold 11 sts on spare needle for

left neck).

Body

Use the intarsia technique and a separate ball of each colour yarn, twisting the colours firmly over one another at the joins to prevent holes forming.

Step 7

Neck and Head

Row 1: With sn and bl, k2sn, k9bl held for neck from spare needle of Right Side of Body, then k9bl, k2sn held for neck from spare needle of Left Side of Body. (22 sts) Join in oc.

Row 2: P2sn, p2oc, p14bl, p2oc, p2sn.

Row 3: K2sn, k2oc, k2togoc, k10bl, k2togoc, k2oc, k2sn. (20 sts)

Row 4: P1sn, p6oc, p6bl, p6oc, p1sn.

Row 5: K1sn, k8oc, k2bl, k8oc, k1sn.

Cont in oc.

Row 6: Purl.

Row 7: K17, wrap and turn (leave 3 sts on left-hand needle unworked).

Row 8: Working top of head on centre 14 sts only, p14, w&t.

Row 9: K14, w&t.

Rep rows 8–9 once more.

Row 12: P14, w&t.

Row 13: Knit across all sts. (20 sts in total) Work 2 rows st st.

Row 16: P2tog, p16, p2tog. (18 sts)

Row 17: K15, w&t (leave 3 sts on left-hand needle unworked).

Join in sn.

Row 18: Working top of head on centre

12 sts only, p5oc, p2sn, p5oc, w&t.

Row 19: K5oc, k2sn, k5oc, w&t.

Rep rows 18–19 once more.

Row 22: P5oc, p2sn, p5oc, w&t.

Row 23: K4oc, k4sn, k7oc. (18 sts in total) Row 24: P4oc, p2togoc, p2sn, p2togsn, p2sn, p2togoc, p4oc. (15 sts)

Row 25: K4oc, k2togsn, k3sn, k2togsn, k4oc. (13 sts)

Row 26: P4oc, p5sn, p4oc. Row 27: K3oc, k7sn, k3oc. Row 28: P2oc, p9sn, p2oc. Cont in sn.

Work 3 rows st st.

Row 32: P2tog, p9, p2tog. (11 sts) Row 33: Knit.

Row 34: P2tog, p7, p2tog. (9 sts) Cast (bind) off.

Step 8

Tail

Use a pipecleaner to stiffen the upright tail.

Tail

Row 1: With bl and with RS facing, k5 held for tail from spare needle of Left Side of Body, then k5 held for tail from spare needle of Right Side of Body. (10 sts)

Row 2: Purl.

Join in oc.

Row 3: K1oc, k8bl, k1oc.

Row 4: P1oc, p8bl, p1oc.

Rep rows 3–4 once more.

Row 7: K2oc, k6bl, k2oc.

Row 8: P2oc, p6bl, p2oc.

Row 9: K3oc, k4bl, k3oc.

Row 10: P3oc, p4bl, p3oc.

Row 11: K2togoc, k2oc, [incbl] twice, k2oc, k2togoc. (10 sts)

Row 12: P3oc, p4bl, p3oc.

Join in sn.

Row 13: K2togsn, k2oc, [incbl] twice, k2oc, k2togsn. (10 sts)

Row 14: P1sn, p3oc, p2bl, p3oc, p1sn. Row 15: K3sn, k4oc, k3sn.

Row 1 6: P4sn, p2oc, p4sn.

Cont in sn.

Row 17: K2tog, k6, k2tog. (8 sts)

Work 3 rows st st.

Row 21: K2tog, k4, k2tog. (6 sts)

Row 22: P2tog, p2, p2tog. (4 sts)

Row 23: [K2tog] twice. (2 sts)

Row 24: P2tog and fasten off.

Step 9

Tummy

With sn, cast on 6 sts. Begwithakrow,work2rowsstst. Row 3: K2tog, k2, k2tog. (4 sts) Work 11 rows st st.

Row 15: Inc, k2, inc. (6 sts)

Work 7 rows st st.

Row 23: Inc, k4, inc. (8 sts)

Work 21 rows st st.

Row 45: K2tog, k4, k2tog. (6 sts) Work 5 rows st st.

Row 51: Inc, k4, inc. (8 sts)

Work 9 rows st st.

Row 61: K2tog, k4, k2tog. (6 sts) Work 17 rows st st.

Row 79: K2tog k2, k2tog. (4 sts) Work 9 rows st st.

Cast (bind) off.

Step 10

Ear

(make 2 the same)

With oc, cast on 4 sts.

Row 1: Inc, k2, inc. (6 sts)

Row 2: Knit.

Row 3: Inc, k4, inc. (8 sts)

Knit 10 rows.

Row 14: K2tog, k4, k2tog. (6 sts) Knit 2 rows.

Row 17: K2tog, k2, k2tog. (4 sts) Knit 2 rows.

Row 20: [K2tog] twice. (2 sts) Cast (bind) off.

Step 11

Collar

With bb, cast on 26 sts. Knit one row.

Cast (bind) off.

Step 12

To Make Up

Sew in ends, leaving ends from cast on and cast (bound) off rows for sewing up.

LEGS With WS together, fold leg in half. Starting at paw, sew up leg on RS.

BODY Sew along back of dog to tail.

TAIL Cut a pipecleaner 2.5cm (1in) longer than tail. Roll a little stuffing around pipecleaner, wrap tail around pipecleaner and sew up tail on RS, sewing down to bottom of bottom. Protruding end of pipecleaner will vanish into body stuffing. HEAD Fold cast (bound) off row of head in half and sew from nose to chin.

TUMMY Sew cast on row of tummy to bottom of dog's bottom (where back legs begin), and sew cast (bound) off row to chin. Ease and sew tummy to fit body, matching curves of tummy to legs. Leave a 2.5cm (1in) gap between front and back legs on one side. STUFFING Pipecleaners are used to stiffen the legs and help bend them into shape. Fold a pipecleaner into a 'U' shape and measure against front two legs. Cut to approximately fit, leaving an extra 2.5cm (1in) at both ends. Fold these ends over to stop pipecleaner poking out of paws. Roll a little stuffing around pipecleaner and slip into body, one end down each front leg. Repeat with second pipecleaner and back legs. Starting at the head, stuff the dog firmly, then sew up the gap. Mould body into shape.

EARS Sew cast on row of each ear to side of dog's head at an angle sloping down towards back, so 4 sts between front of ears, 10 sts between back of ears.

EYES With bl, sew 2-loop French knots positioned as in photograph.

NOSE With bl, embroider nose in satin stitch. COLLAR Sew ends of collar together and pop over head.

Golden Retriever

The Golden Retriever is made in smooth yarn that loops beautifully.

You Will Need

- Tiny amount of Rowan Pure 4ply Wool in Black 404 (bl) for eyes and nose

- 2 Pipe Cleaner(s) for legs

- Small amount of Rowan Cashsoft Yarn 4ply in Toxic 459 (tx) for collar

- 23?4mm (US 2) Double Pointed Knitting Needles (for holding stitches)

- 30g (11?4oz) of Rowan Creative Focus Worsted Yarn in Camel 02132 (ca)

- Pair of 23?4mm (US 2) Knitting Needles

Step 1

Right Back Leg

With ca, cast on 7 sts.

Beg with a k row, work 2 rows st st.

Row 3: Inc, k2tog, k1, k2tog, inc. (7 sts) Work 7 rows st st.

Row 11: K1, inc, k1, inc, k1, inc, k1. (10 sts) Row 12 and every alt row: Purl.

Row 13: K2tog, inc, loopy st 1, k2, loopy st 1, inc, k2tog. (10 sts)

Row 15: K2, [inc] twice, k2, [inc] twice, k2. (14 sts)

Row 17: K1, loopy st 1, k1, [inc] twice, k4, [inc] twice, k1, loopy st 1, k1. (18 sts)

Row 19: K3, inc, k10, inc, k3. (20 sts)

Row 21: K1, loopy st 1, k1, inc, k12, inc, k1, loopy st 1, k1. (22 sts)

Row 23: K3, inc, k14, inc, k3. (24 sts)

Row 25: K1, loopy st 1, k20, loopy st 1, k1.* Row 27: Cast (bind) off 12 sts, k to end (hold 12 sts on spare needle for Right Side of Body).\

Step 2

Left Back Leg

Work as for Right Back Leg to *.

Row 26: Purl.

Row 27: K12, cast (bind) off 12 sts (hold 12 sts on spare needle for Left Side of Body).

Step 3

Right Front Leg

With ca, cast on 7 sts.

Beg with a k row, work 2 rows st st.

Row 3: Inc, k2tog, k1, k2tog, inc. (7 sts) Work 3 rows st st.

Row 7: Inc, k5, inc. (9 sts)

Work 3 rows st st.

Row 11: K1, loopy st 1, k5, loopy st 1, k1. Work 3 rows st st.

Row 15: K1, loopy st 1, k5, loopy st 1, k1. Work 3 rows st st.

Row 19: Inc, loopy st 1, k5, loopy st 1, inc. (11 sts)

Row 20: Purl.**

Row 21: Cast (bind) off 5 sts, k to end (hold 6 sts on spare needle for Right Side of Body).

Step 4

Left Front Leg

Work as for Right Front Leg to **.

Row 21: K6, cast (bind) off 5 sts (hold 6 sts on spare needle for Left Side of Body).

Step 5

Right Side of Body

Row 1: With ca, cast on 1 st, with RS facing k6 from spare needle of Right Front Leg, cast on 3 sts. (10 sts)

Row 2: Purl.

Row 3: K10, cast on 4 sts. (14 sts) Row 4: Purl.

Row 5: Inc, k13, cast on 3 sts. (18 sts) Row 6: Purl.

Row 7: K18, cast on 4 sts. (22 sts)

Row 8: Purl.

Row 9: K22, with RS facing k12 from spare needle of Right Back Leg. (34 sts)

Work 5 rows st st.

Row 15: K32, k2tog. (33 sts)

Row 16: Purl.

Row 17: K31, k2tog. (32 sts)

Row 18: Purl.

Row 19: K30, k2tog. (31 sts)

Row 20: Purl.

Row 21: K29, k2tog. (30 sts)

Row 22: Cast (bind) off 21 sts, p to end (hold 9 sts on spare needle for right neck).

Step 6

Left Side of Body

Row 1: With ca, cast on 1 st, with WS facing p6 from spare needle of Left Front Leg, cast on 3 sts. (10 sts)

Row 2: Knit.

Row 3: P10, cast on 4 sts. (14 sts) Row 4: Knit.

Row 5: Inc, p13, cast on 3 sts. (18 sts) Row 6: Knit.

Row 7: P18, cast on 4 sts. (22 sts)

Row 8: Knit.

Row 9: P22, with WS facing p12 from spare needle of Left Back Leg. (34 sts)

Work 5 rows st st.

Row 15: P32, p2tog. (33 sts)

Row 16: Knit.

Row 17: P31, p2tog. (32 sts)

Row 18: Knit.

Row 19: P30, p2tog. (31 sts)

Row 20: Knit.

Row 21: P29, p2tog. (30 sts)

Row 22: Cast (bind) off 21 sts, k to end (hold 9 sts on spare needle for left neck).

Step 7

Neck and Head

Row 1: With ca and with RS facing, k9 held for neck from spare needle of Right Side of Body, then k9 held for neck from spare needle of Left Side of Body. (18 sts)

Row 2: Purl.

Row 3: Knit.

Row 4: Purl.

Row 5: Inc, k16, inc. (20 sts) Row 6: Purl.

Row 7: K17, wrap and turn (leave 3 sts on left-hand needle unworked).

Row 8: Working top of head on centre 14 sts only, p14, w&t.

Row 9: K14, w&t.

Row 10: P14, w&t.

Row 11: K14, w&t.

Row 12: P14, w&t.

Row 13: Knit across all sts. (20 sts in total) Work 3 rows st st.

Row 17: K16, w&t (leave 4 sts on left-hand needle unworked).

Row 18: Working top of head on centre 12 sts only, p12, w&t.

Row 19: K12, w&t.

Row 20: P12, w&t.

Row 21: K12, w&t.

Row 22: P12, w&t.

Row 23: Knit across all sts. (20 sts in total) Row 24: Purl.

Row 25: K4, [k2tog] twice, k4, [k2tog] twice, k4. (16 sts)

Row 26: Purl.

Row 27: K4, k2tog, k4, k2tog, k4. (14 sts) Row 28: Purl.

Row 29: K3, k2tog, k4, k2tog, k3. (12 sts) Work 3 rows st st.

Row 33: K2tog, k8, k2tog. (10 sts)

Row 34: Purl.

Cast (bind) off.

Step 8

Tail

The Retriever has quite a muscular tail as it's a great wagger.

Tail

With ca, cast on 1 st. Row 1: Inc. (2 sts)

Row 2: Purl.

Row 3: [Inc] twice. (4 sts) Row 4: Purl.

Row 5: K1, inc, k2. (5 sts) Row 6: Purl.

Row 7: K2, loopy st 1, k2. Row 8: Purl.

Row 9: Knit.

Row 10: Purl.

Rep rows 7–10 twice more.

Row 19: Inc, k1, loopy st 1, k1, inc. (7 sts) Work 3 rows st st.

Row 23: K3, loopy st 1, k3.

Row 24: Purl.

Row 25: Knit.

Row 26: Purl.

Rep rows 23–26 once more.

Row 31: K3, loopy st 1, k3.

Row 32: Purl.

Cast (bind) off.

Step 9

Tummy

With ca, cast on 1 st. Row 1: Inc. (2 sts)

Row 2: [Inc] twice. (4 sts) Row 3: Inc, k2, inc. (6 sts) Row 4: Inc, p4, inc. (8 sts) Work 18 rows st st.

Row 23: K3, loopy st 2, k3. Row 24: Purl.

Row 25: Knit.

Row 26: Purl.

Rep rows 23–26, 6 times more. Row 51: K1, loopy st 6, k1. Row 52: Purl.

Row 53: Knit.

Row 54: Purl.

Rep rows 51–54 once more.

Row 59: K2tog, loopy st 4, k2tog. (6 sts) Work 3 rows st st.

Row 63: K1, loopy st 4, k1.

Work 15 rows st st.

Row 79: K2tog, k2, k2tog. (4 sts) Work 11 rows st st.

Row 91: [K2tog] twice. (2 sts) Row 92: Purl.

Row 93: K2tog and fasten off.

Step 10

Ear

(make 2 the same)

With ca, cast on 7 sts.

Beg with a k row, work 5 rows st st. Row 6: P2tog, p3, p2tog. (5 sts) Row 7: K2tog, k1, k2tog. (3 sts) Row 8: Purl.

Row 9: K3tog and fasten off.

Step 11

Head

Stuff the nose carefully so there is a nice curve to the chin.

Collar

With tx, cast on 30 sts. Knit one row.

Cast (bind) off.

Step 12

To Make Up

SEWING IN ENDS Sew in ends, leaving ends from cast on and cast (bound) off rows for sewing up.

LEGS With WS together, fold leg in half. Starting at paw, sew up leg on RS.

BODY Sew along back of dog and 2cm (3⁄4in) down bottom.

HEAD Fold cast (bound) off row of head in half and sew from nose to chin.

TUMMY Sew cast on row of tummy to where you have finished sewing down bottom, and sew cast (bound) off row to chin. Ease and sew tummy to fit body. Leave a 2.5cm (1in) gap between front and back legs on one side. STUFFING Pipecleaners are used to stiffen the legs and help bend them into shape. Fold a pipecleaner into a 'U' shape and measure against front two legs. Cut to approximately fit, leaving an extra 2.5cm (1in) at both ends. Fold these ends over to stop pipecleaner poking out of paws. Roll a little stuffing around pipecleaner and slip into body, one end down each front leg. Repeat with second pipecleaner and back legs. Starting at the head, stuff the dog firmly, then sew up the gap. Mould body into shape.

TAIL Sew up tail on RS and sew to dog where back meets bottom, with loops on underside.

EARS Sew cast on row of each ear to side of dog's head, with wrong side of ears facing downwards. Attach at an angle sloping down towards back, so 6 sts between front of ears, 10 sts between back of ears.

EYES With bl, sew 2-loop French knots with 1 tiny straight stitch on the outside, positioned as in photograph.

NOSE With bl, embroider nose in satin stitch. COLLAR Sew ends of collar together and pop over head.

Shar Pei

The Shar Pei has wrinkly skin and you can, if you like, add more wrinkles to your dog.

You Will Need

- 3 Pipe Cleaner(s) for legs and tail
- Tiny amount of Rowan Pure Wool 4ply in Black 404 (bl) for eyes and nose
- Small amount of Rowan Cashsoft 4ply Yarn in Toxic 459 (tx) for collar
- 5g (1?8oz) of Rowan Pure 4ply Wool in Mocha 417 (mo)
- 30g (11?4oz) of Rowan Pure 4ply Wool in Toffee 453 (to)
- Pair of 23?4mm (US 2) Knitting Needles

- 23?4mm (US 2) Double Pointed Knitting Needles (for holding stitches)

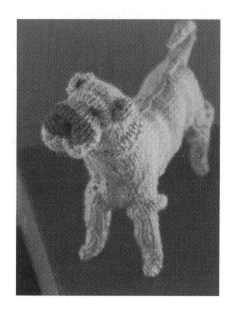

Step 1

Right Back Leg

With to, cast on 6 sts.

Beg with a k row, work 2 rows st st.

Row 3: Inc, k1, k2tog, k1, inc. (7 sts)

Row 4: Purl.

Row 5: Inc, k2tog, k1, k2tog, inc. (7 sts) Work 9 rows st st.

Row 15: K2tog, inc, k1, inc, k2tog. (7 sts) Row 16: Purl.

Row 17: K1, inc, k3, inc, k1. (9 sts)

Row 18: Purl.

Row 19: K1, inc, k5, inc, k1. (11 sts)

Row 20: Purl.

Row 21: K1, inc, k7, inc, k1. (13 sts)

Row 22: Purl.

Row 23: K1, inc, k4, inc, k4, inc, k1. (16 sts) Row 24: Purl.

Row 25: K1, inc, k12, inc, k1. (18 sts)

Row 26: Purl.

Work 5 rows st st.

Row 32: To make a wrinkle, *pick up st from row 26, p2tog (st on needle and st picked up), p1, rep from * to end of row.**

Row 33: Cast (bind) off 9 sts, k to end (hold 9 sts on spare needle for Right Side of Body).

Step 2

Left Back Leg

Work as for Right Back Leg to **.

Row 33: K9, cast (bind) off 9 sts (hold 9 sts on spare needle for Left Side of Body).

Step 3

Right Front Leg

With to, cast on 6 sts.

Beg with a k row, work 2 rows st st. Row 3: Inc, [k2tog] twice, inc. (6 sts) Row 4: Purl.

Row 5: K2, [inc] twice, k2. (8 sts) Work 7 rows st st.

Row 13: K1, inc, k4, inc, k1. (10 sts) Row 14: Purl.

Work 2 rows st st.

Row 17: K1, inc, k6, inc, k1. (12 sts) Row 18: Purl.

Row 19: K1, inc, k8, inc, k1. (14 sts)

Row 20: Purl.

Row 21: K1, inc, k10, inc, k1. (16 sts)

Work 4 rows st st.

Row 26: To make a wrinkle, *pick up st from row 21, p2tog (st on needle and st picked up), p1, rep from * to end of row.***

Row 27: Cast (bind) off 8 sts, k to end (hold 8 sts on spare needle for Right Side of Body).

Step 4

Left Front Leg

Work as for Right Front Leg to ***.

Row 27: K8, cast (bind) off 8 sts (leave 8 sts on spare needle for Left Side of Body).

Step 5

Right Side of Body

Row 1: With to, cast on 1 st, with RS facing k8 from spare needle of Right Front Leg, cast on 6 sts. (15 sts)

Row 2: Purl.

Row 3: K15, cast on 6 sts. (21 sts)

Row 4: Purl.

Row 5: Inc, k20, cast on 8 sts, with RS facing k9 from spare needle of Right Back Leg. (39 sts)

Work 5 rows st st.

Row 11: Inc, k38. (40 sts)

Work 4 rows st st.

Row 16: P2tog, p37, inc. (40 sts)

Row 17: K14, cast (bind) off 12 sts, k to end. Work on last set of 14 sts.

Row 18: P14.

Row 19: Cast (bind) off 9 sts, k to end (hold 5 sts on spare needle for tail).

Row 20: With WS facing rejoin yarn to rem sts, p2tog, p12. (13 sts)

Row 21: K11, k2tog. (12 sts)

Row 22: P2tog, p10 (hold 11 sts on spare needle for right neck).

Body

For more wrinkles, add an extra six rows and pick up as for other wrinkles

Step 6

Left Side of Body

Row 1: With to, cast on 1 st, with WS facing p8 from spare needle of Left Front Leg, cast on 6 sts. (15 sts)

Row 2: Knit.

Row 3: P15, cast on 6 sts. (21 sts)

Row 4: Knit.

Row 5: Inc, p20, cast on 8 sts, with WS facing p9 from spare needle of Left Back Leg. (39 sts)

Work 5 rows st st.

Row 11: Inc, p38. (40 sts)

Work 4 rows st st.

Row 16: K2tog, k37, inc. (40 sts)

Row 17: P14, cast (bind) off 12 sts, p to end. Work on last set of 14 sts.

Row 18: K14.

Row 19: Cast (bind) off 9 sts, p to end (hold 5 sts on spare needle for tail).

Row 20: With RS facing rejoin yarn to rem sts, k2tog, k12. (13 sts)

Row 21: P11, p2tog. (12 sts)

Row 22: K2tog, k10 (hold 11 sts on spare needle for left neck).

Step 7

Neck and Head

Row 1: With to and with RS facing, k11 held for neck from spare needle of Right Side of Body, then k11 held for neck from spare needle of Left Side of Body. (22 sts)

Row 2: Purl.

Work 5 rows st st.

Row 8: To make a wrinkle, *pick up st from row 2, p2tog (st on needle and st picked up), p1, rep from * to end of row.

Row 9: Knit.

Row 10: P1, p2tog, p16, p2tog, p1. (20 sts) Row 11: Knit.

Row 12: P1, p2tog, p14, p2tog, p1. (18 sts) Row 13: K15, wrap and turn (leave 3 sts on left-hand needle unworked).

Row 14: P12, w&t.

Row 15: Working top of head on centre

12 sts only, k12, w&t.

Row 16: P12, w&t.

Row 17: Knit across all sts. (18 sts in total) Row 18: Purl.

Row 19: K14, w&t (leave 4 sts on left-hand needle unworked).

ow 20: P10, w&t.

Row 21: Working top of head on centre

10 sts only, k10, w&t.

Row 22: P10, w&t.

Row 23: Knit across all sts. (18 sts in total) Row 24: P2, [p2tog] 3 times, p2, [p2tog]

3 times, p2. (12 sts)

Work 5 rows st st.

Row 30: To make a wrinkle, *pick up st from row 24, [p2tog (st on needle and st picked up)] 4 times*, p4, rep from * to * once more. Work 2 rows st st.

Join in mo.

Row 33: K2to, k8mo, k2to.

Row 34: P2to, p8mo, p2to.

Rep rows 33–34 once more.

Row 37: K3to, k6mo, k3to.

Row 38: P3to, p6mo, p3to.

Rep rows 37–38 twice more.

Row 43: K2togto, k2to, k4mo, k2to, k2togto. (10 sts)

Row 44: P2togto, p2to, p2mo, p2to, p2togto. (8 sts)

Cast (bind) off 8 sts.

Step 8

Tail

Row 1: With to and with RS facing, k5 held for tail from spare needle of Left Side of Body, then k5 held for tail from spare needle of Right Side of Body. (10 sts)

Beg with a p row, work 3 rows st st. Row 5: K2tog, k6, k2tog. (8 sts) Work 3 rows st st.

Row 9: K2tog, k4, k2tog. (6 sts) Work 7 rows st st.

Row 17: K2tog, k2, k2tog. (4 sts) Work 3 rows st st.

Row 21: [K2tog] twice. (2 sts) Row 22: P2tog and fasten off.

Step 9

Tummy

With to, cast on 1 st. Row 1: Inc. (2 sts)

Row 2: Purl.

Row 3: [Inc] twice. (4 sts) Row 4: Purl.

Row 5: Inc, k2, inc. (6 sts) Row 6: Purl.

Row 7: Inc, k4, inc. (8 sts) Work 61 rows st st.

Row 69: K2tog, k4, k2tog. (6 sts) Work 39 rows st st.

Cast (bind) off.

Step 10

Ear

(make 2 the same)

With to, cast on 6 sts.

Work 4 rows st st.

Row 5: K2tog, k2, k2tog. (4 sts) Row 6: Purl.

Row 7: [K2tog] twice. (2 sts) Row 8: P2tog and fasten off.

Step 11

Collar

With tx, cast on 30 sts. Knit one row.

Cast (bind) off.

Step 12

To Make Up

SEWING IN ENDS Sew in ends, leaving ends from cast on and cast (bound) off rows for sewing up.

LEGS With WS together, fold leg in half. Starting at paw, sew up leg on RS.

BODY Sew along back of dog to tail.

TAIL Cut a pipecleaner 2.5cm (1in) longer than tail. Roll a little stuffing around pipecleaner, wrap tail around pipecleaner and sew up tail on RS, sewing down to just below root of tail. Protruding end of pipecleaner will vanish into body stuffing. Bend tail over back.

HEAD Fold cast (bound) off row of head in half and sew from nose to chin. Stuff head lightly. Thread tapestry needle with toffee yarn and fasten end to tip of nose. Take thread through head to emerge at top back (see diagrams on page 173), and pull up to form wrinkles. Fold nose in on itself to form jowls and sew centre of jowls to end of muzzle in middle of mo section.

TUMMY Sew cast on row of tummy to where you have finished sewing down bottom, and sew cast (bound) off row to chin. Ease and sew tummy to fit body. Leave a 2.5cm (1in) gap between front and back legs on one side. STUFFING Pipecleaners are used to stiffen the legs and help bend them into shape. Fold a pipecleaner into a 'U' shape and measure against front two legs. Cut to approximately fit, leaving an extra 2.5cm (1in) at both ends. Fold these ends over to stop pipecleaner poking out of paws. Roll a little stuffing around pipecleaner and slip into body, one end down each front leg. Repeat with second pipecleaner and back legs. Starting at the head, stuff the dog firmly, then sew up the gap. Sew up neck wrinkle across chest. Mould body into shape. If you want your dog to be more wrinkly, run a strand of toffee yarn from nose to bottom and back and pull up slightly for concertina effect.

EARS Sew cast on row of each ear to side of dog's head, following natural slope of head and with 5 sts between ears and with wrong side of ears facing downwards. Catch ears down with a stitch.

EYES With bl, sew 2 short horizontal satin stitches in front of large head wrinkle, as

in photograph.

NOSE With bl, embroider nose in satin stitch. COLLAR Sew ends of collar together and pop over head.

Chico The Chihuahua

Safety guidelines

The items in these patterns are not suitable for babies and

very young children.

Knitting yarns

Small oddments of Double knitting in various colours, as stated in the instructions

Abbreviations

P - Purl. P1 - Purl one. Pwise - Purl Wise.

K - Knit. K1 - Knit one. Kwise - Knit Wise

Sts - stitches,

K2 tog - Knit 2 Together. P2 tog - Purl 2 Together.

Inc 1 - Increase 1 stitch. Y.Fwd - Yarn forward around needle.

St-st - Stocking Stitch. G-st - Garter stitch,

B+T tightly - Break off yarn leaving a long end and thread it through stitches left on knitting needle, pull together tightly then fasten off.

Additional instructions - for some of the detailing you will need to be able to make a chain stitch.

For This Project - You need.

Knitting yarns.

Fawn for Chico

Red for his coat

Additional materials.

Toy eyes

Embroidery thread in Black

Toy Stuffing – Small bag.

Tools.

No.10 needles. UK sized

Wool needle. UK sized

Sewing needle.

Scissors.

Front legs, neck and head. (One piece)

Cast on 4 Sts on No.10 needles in Beige.

KW Inc1 into every st

P 1 row

KW Inc1 into every st

p 1 row

St st 2 rows.

(K1, K2tog) to last 2 sts, K2tog

St st 13 rows.

Put this aside on a needle and make a second leg in the exact same way.

Once you have both legs done, put on one needle.

Put both sets of stitches on one needle with right side facing, then knit across both legs to join.

St st 10 rows.

Next row -***P2tog, P to last 2 sts , P2tog.

K1 row**.

Repeat from *** to ** until 14 Sts remain.

Do not K the last row

Increase for the head as follows.

K1, (Inc 1, K1), K1

P 1 row. (20 Sts)

(K1, Inc1) to end

St st 11 rows.

Next row - (K3, K2tog) to end.

Next row - (P2, P2tog) to end.

Next row - (K1, K2tog) to end.

P2 tog to end.

B+T tightly.

To make up

Sew from top of the head, down to where the neck is and stuff. Draw a little wool through the increase for head row and pull tight for neck (using an in and out stitch around the neck and pulling a little tighter to draw in).

Sew down body and stuff as you go to the point where legs begin.

Sew legs from joint between legs down each and stuff leaving bases of the feet open. There will be a flat line down back of head this is normal

Leave this piece aside for now

Back legs and rump.

Leg (Make 2)

Cast on 4 Sts on No.10 needles in Beige.

KW Inc1 into every st

P 1 row

KW Inc1 into every st

St st 3 rows.

(K1, K2tog) to end

St st 13 rows.

Once second piece is knitted put both sets of stitches on one needle (20 sts) right side facing and K across both legs

Next row - St st 10 rows

Next row - (P3, P2tog) to end

Next row - (K1, K2tog) to end

Next row - (P2tog) to end, P1

B+t tightly

To make up

Draw thread tightly and sew down to where legs meet, stuff well.

Join legs and sew down each one, stuffing and leaving bases open.

Middle section of body

Cast on 15 Sts on No.10 needles in Fawn

St st until work measures 7.5 cm. Approx 32 rows.

Cast off.

To make up

Sew cast off edge to cast on edge, making a tube shape. Stuff lightly to hold

shape and sew back legs to one open end and front legs to other - making

sure the seams are facing into the tube on both pieces, and the stomach

seam faces down. Add more stuffing before closing completely, to stiffen.

This is quite tricky to sew together and you may find using safety pins to

hold in place while sewing helpful.

Ears (make 2)

Cast on 10 Sts

P 1 row

KW Inc 1 in every st.

P 1 row

Next row - K4, K2tog, to last K2.

P 1 row

Next row - K3, K2tog, to last 2 P 1 row

Next row - K2, K2tog to last 2 P 1 row

Next row - (P1, P2tog to last 2 P 1 row

Next row - (K2 tog) to end.

P 1 row

K2tog, twice B+T tightly.

To make up

Fold in half and flatten to make a triangle shape. Sew up seam, move seam to center back, gather base in the center to pinch ear before sewing to dogs head at each side. Position is optional. Sew in place.

Muzzle

Cast on 15 Sts on No.12 needles in White.

K 1 row.

P2tog, P to last 2 sts, P2 tog.

K 1 row.

Repeat these last 2 rows until 9 Sts remain, ending on K row.

P2tog to end, P1

B+T tightly.

Draw tightly to close the end, sew up side seam. Stuff lightly and sew onto front of Unicorns face. Leave enough space on the upper part of face for eyes and fringe.

Tail

Cast on 6sts

Stst 20 rows

K2tog to end

B+T

Sew seams up without stuffing the tail, gather base to close and sew to dogs rump.

Coat

In red Cast on 20 stst

K 2 rows

K2, P to last 2 sts, K2

K 1 row

Repeat last 2 rows, 7 more times

K2, P4, cast off 8 sts, P4, K2

Work on first 6 sts

K4, K2 tog

P2tog, P1, K2

K 1 row

P2, K2

Repeat last 2 rows, 5 more times

Cast off

Rejoin to last 6 sts

K2tog, K4

K2, P1, P2tog

K1 row

K2, P2

Repeat last 2 rows, 5 more times

Cast off

Belly strap

Cast on 10sts in red

Stst 2 rows

Cast off

The coat lays on dogs back with the two front straps pulled around and overlapping at the front. Stitch or add a closure if you want it to be removable.

The belly strap is sewn at each center side as pictured. Make one side with a button or closure if you want it to come off. Mine is sewn in place.

My Precious Puppy

What you will need:

- RED HEART® Boutique Fur™: 2 balls 9406 Smoke A

- RED HEART® Super Saver®: 1 skein

- Each of, 400 Grey Heather B, 312 Black C, 706 Perfect Pink D.

Note: Only small amounts of B, C, and D are needed

Susan Bates® Knitting Needles:

- 12.75mm [US 17] and 4mm [US 6]

- Stuffing, yarn needle

GAUGE: 4 sts = 4" (10 cm) in Garter stitch (knit every row) using larger needles and A. CHECK YOUR GAUGE. Use any size needles to obtain the gauge.

Puppy measures about 7" [18 cm] tall and 10½" [26.5 cm] long.

Notes

1. Body, head, legs, ears, and tail are worked with larger needles and Fur yarn.

2. Snout, nose, tongue, and eyes are worked with smaller needles and Super Saver.

3. All pieces are sewn together with yarn needle and B.

Special Stitch

kfb (Knit into front and back) = Knit next st but do not remove from needle, knit into back loop of same st and remove from needle.

BODY

With larger needles and A, cast on 3 sts.

Row 1: Kfb in each st across—6 sts.

Row 2: Knit.

Row 3: [K1, kfb] 3 times—9 sts.

Row 4: Knit.

Row 5: [K2, kfb] 3 times—12 sts.

Rows 6–8: Knit.

Row 9: [K2, k2tog] 3 times——9 sts.

Row 10: Knit.

Row 11: [K1, k2tog] 3 times——6 sts.

Bind off.

Finishing Body: Thread a length of B onto yarn needle and weave through stitches of bound-off edge, pull tight to gather.

Sew side edges together for bottom seam, stuffing piece before completing seam.

Weave B through stitches of cast-on edge and pull tight to gather. Weave in end securely.

HEAD

With larger needles and A, cast on 3 sts.

Row 1: Kfb in each st across——6 sts.

Row 2: Knit.

Row 3: [K1, kfb] 3 times—9 sts.

Rows 4–6: Knit.

Row 7: [K1, k2tog] 3 times—6 sts.

Row 8: Knit.

Bind off.

Finishing Head: Finish same as body.

FRONT LEG (make 2)

With larger needles and A, cast on 4 sts.

Rows 1–4: Knit.

Bind off.

Finishing Front Leg: Finish same as body, stuffing firmly.

BACK LEG (make 2)

Beginning at lower end (paw), with larger needles and A, cast on 3 sts.

Row 1: Kfb in each st across—6 sts.

Rows 2–4: Knit.

Bind off.

Finishing Back Leg: Thread a length of B onto yarn needle and weave through stitches of cast-on edge, pull tight to gather.

Sew side edges together for bottom seam, stuffing piece before completing seam. Do not gather bound-off edge, hold work flat and sew edges of bound-off edges together.

Weave in end securely.

EAR (make 2)

With larger needles and A, cast on 3 sts.

Rows 1–3: Knit.

Bind off.

TAIL

With larger needles and A, cast on 3 sts.

Rows 1–3: Knit.

Bind off.

SNOUT

Beginning at tip of snout, with smaller needles and B, cast on 3 sts.

Row 1: Kfb in each st across—6 sts.

Row 2: Purl.

Row 3: Kfb in each st across—12 sts.

Row 4: Purl.

Row 5: [K1, kfb] 6 times—18 sts.

Row 6: Knit.

Rows 7 and 8: Purl.

Bind off, leaving a long tail for sewing. Sew side seam, leaving Row 8 open. Stuff and sew in place on front of head.

NOSE

Beginning at top of nose, with smaller needles and C, cast on 5 sts.

Rows 1 and 2: Knit.

Row 3: K2tog, k1, k2tog—3 sts.

Row 4: Knit.

Row 5: K3tog—1 st.

Fasten off remaining stitch, leaving a long tail for sewing. Sew in place on tip of snout. With C, using photograph as a

guide, embroider straight stitches for mouth, below nose.

TONGUE

Beginning at top of nose, with smaller needles and D, cast on 3 sts.

Rows 1 and 2: Knit.

Row 3: K3tog—1 st.

Fasten off remaining stitch, leaving a long tail for sewing. Sew tongue to snout at embroidered mouth.

EYE (make 2)

With smaller needles and B, cast on 3 sts.

Row 1: Kfb, k1, kfb—5 sts.

Row 2: K2tog, k1, k2tog—3 sts.

Row 3: K3tog—1 st.

Fasten off remaining stitch, leaving a long tail. Thread tail onto yarn needle and weave tail in and out of outer edge, pull to gather.

Sew eyes to front of head above snout.

FINISHING

Assembly: Refer to photograph for placement of all pieces. With yarn needle and B, sew ears to top of head. Sew head to top of one end of body, sewing around head a couple of times and making sure that you sew through the stitches (not just the outer layer of fur). Sew front legs as if puppy is standing, sewing firmly in place. Sew back legs horizontally as if puppy is sitting,

sewing firmly in place. Sew tail to back end of body.

Weave in any remaining ends.

ABBREVIATIONS

A, B, C, and D = Color A, Color B, Color C, and Color D; k = knit; k2tog = knit next 2 sts together; k3tog = knit next 3 sts together; st(s) = stitch(es); [ ] = work directions in brackets the number of times specified.

A Floppy Dog

Size: Approx. 31 cm (12 in) tall

Materials:

- 250 g (1¾ oz) balls of Jaeger Baby Merino DK in main colour M (soft grey/Flannel 228) and 1 ball in C (pale brown/Choco 188)
- Pair of 3.25 mm (US 3) knitting needles
- Knitter's sewing needle
- Washable stuffing
- Embroidery needle
- Pink velvet ribbon

Tension/gauge

26 sts and 36 rows to 10 cm (4 in) square over stocking/stockinette stitch using 3.25 mm (US 3) needles.

Body and head

Start at lower edge

Using M, cast on 20sts.

1st row (WS) and alt rows P.

2nd row K4, m1, k2, m1, (k4, m1) twice, k2, m1, k4. (25sts)

4th row K1, m1, k4, m1, k2, m1, k5, m1, k1, m1, k5, m1, k2, m1, k4, m1, k1. (33sts)

6th row K.

8th row K7, m1, k2, m1, k15, m1, k2, m1, k7. (37sts)

10th row K.

12th row K2, m1, k6, m1, k2, m1, k7, m1, k3, m1, k7, m1, k2, m1, k6, m1, k2. (45sts)

13th-17th rows Stocking/stockinette stitch.

Body patch

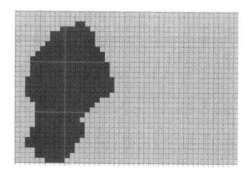

Using stocking/stockinette stitch and intarsia technique, work 1st-29th rows from body patch chart.

Shape top of body

1st row (K3, k2tog) twice, k2, (skpo, k3) twice, k1, (k3, k2tog) twice, k2, (skpo, k3) twice. (37sts)

2nd-4th rows Stocking/stockinette stitch.

5th row (K2, k2tog) twice, k2, (skpo, k2) twice, k1, (k2, k2tog) twice, k2, (skpo, k2) twice. (29sts)

6th-8th rows Stocking/stockinette stitch.

Shape head

1. 1st row (K2, m1, k3, m1) twice, k3, m1, (k1, m1) three times, k3, (m1, k3, m1, k2) twice. (41sts)
2. 2nd row P.
3. 3rd row K18, m1, k2, m1, k1, m1, k2, m1, k18. (45sts)
4. 4th-10th rows Stocking/stockinette stitch.
5. 11th row K19, k2tog, k3, skpo, k19.
6. 12th row P18, p2togb, p3, p2tog, p18.
7. 13th row K17, k2tog, k3, skpo, k17.
8. 14th row P.
9. 15th row K16, k2tog, k3, skpo, k16. (37sts)
10. 16th row P.

Eye patch

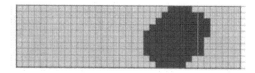

Using stocking/stockinette stitch and intarsia technique, work 1st-10th rows from eye patch chart.

27th row K1, (k3, k2tog) 7 times, k1.

28th row P.

29th row K1, (k2, k2tog) 7 times, k1.

30th row P.

31st row K1, (k1, k2tog) 7 times, k1.

32nd row (P2tog) 8 times.

Break yarn, leaving a length for sewing. Thread yarn through remaining sts, pull together and secure firmly. With RS together, sew back seam leaving cast on edge open.

Feet and legs

Start at foot.

Using M, cast on 30 sts.

1. 1st row (Inc, k13, inc) twice.
2. 2nd row P.
3. 3rd row (Inc, k15, inc) twice. (38sts)

4. 4th-8th rows Stocking/stockinette stitch.

5. 9th row K15, (skpo) twice, (k2tog) twice, k15.

6. 10th row P.

7. 11th row K11, (skpo) three times, (k2tog) three times, k11.

8. 12th row P.

9. 13th row K8, (skpo) three times, (k2tog) three times, k8. (22sts)

10.   14th-36th rows Stocking/stockinette stitch.

11.   Cast/bind off.

12.   Make second foot and leg to match.

Arms (make 2)

Using M, cast on 8sts.

1. 1st row (Inc, k1) 4 times.

2. 2nd row P.

3. 3rd row (K2, m1) twice, k4, (m1, k2) twice.

4. 4th row P.

5. 5th row (K3, m1) twice, k4, (m1, k3) twice. (20sts)

6. 6th-30th rows Stocking/stockinette stitch.

70

7. 31st and 32nd rows Cast/bind off 3sts, work to end.

8. 33rd-35th rows Dec each end.

9. 36th row P.

10.   Cast/bind off.

11.   Make second arm to match.

Ears

Using M, cast on 8sts.

1. Work 48 rows in stocking/stockinette stitch, inc each end of 3rd and 7th rows, dec each end of 21st, 23rd and 24th rows, inc each end of 26th, 27th and 29th rows and dec each end of 43rd and 47th rows.

2. Cast/bind off.

3. Make second ear to match.

Tail

Using M, cast on 12sts.

Work 16 rows in stocking/stockinette stitch.

1. 17th row K2tog, k3, (inc) twice, k3, k2tog.

71

2. 18th row P.

3. 19th-22nd rows Work as 17th-18th rows, twice. (12sts)

4. 23rd row K2tog, knit to last 2sts, k2tog.

5. 24th row P.

6. 25th-30th rows Work as 23rd?24th rows, 3 times. (4sts)

7. 31st row (K2tog) twice.

8. 32nd row P2tog, fasten off.

Finishing

Weave in any loose ends.

Legs

With RS together, join leg and foot seam. Turn RS out and stuff lightly to give floppy effect, close cast/bound off edge.

Arms

With RS together, join arm seam. Turn RS out and stuff lightly to give floppy effect.

Body

Stuff lightly to give floppy effect and close lower edge, make sure that seam to head is at centre back. Attach legs to lower edge. Attach arms to body, adding stuffing if necessary.

Ears

Fold ear in half, RS together and sew side seams. Turn RS out. Attach to head.

Tail

With RS together sew seam. Turn RS out and stuff. Close opening and attach to back seam.

Embroider face, see photograph. Tie ribbon around neck and stitch in place if preferred.

Rufus The Lab Puppy

Finished measurements

Height: approximately 8 inches / 20 cms to the tip of the ears

Length : approximately 12 inches / 30 cms

from the nose to the point of the tail

Width: approximately 3 inches / 7.5 cms

Materials

- Approximately 120 yards of worsted weight yarn. I used Cloudborn Fibers yarn Superwash Merino Worsted Twist in Oatmeal Heather (221 yards / 100 g)
- 1 set of US #5 (3.75 mm) double pointed needles
- US #7 (4.5 mm) needles (for knitting the ears)
- Toy stuffing
- Sew-on doll's eyes size 10mm
- Tapestry needle
- Stitch marker

Gauge

5.75 sts / 8 rows = 1 inches in stockinette stitch.

Note : gauge is not critical for this project.

Pattern notes

In this project I explained the methods I used to knit the puppies, but feel free to use other methods as long as they can achieve the same results.

Casting on (CO)

Judy's Magic Cast On

I used this for starting the snout.

Increase

Throughout the project I used the "backward loop m1" method, recommended by Elizabeth Zimmerman because of the simplicity and invisibility.

Decrease

ssk : slip 2 stitches as if to knit, then knit those 2 stitches together

k2tog : knit 2 stitches together

sk2p : slip stitch as if to knit, k2tog, then pass the slipped stitch over

Short Row

w&t (wrap and turn)

On a knit row: slip the next stitch purlwise, bring the yarn to the front of the work, and replace the slipped stitch back onto the left needle without twisting it. Turn the work around to begin working back in the other direction.

On a purl row: slip the next stitch purlwise, bring the yarn to the back of the work, and replace the slipped stitch back onto the left needle without twisting it. Turn the work around to begin working back in the other direction.

Directions

Main Body and Head

The body is knitted continuously from the snout to the back.

Make Judy's Magic Cast On 16 sts, 8 on each needle.

Round 1 K. 16 sts.

Round 2 K1, m1, k6, m1, k2, m1, k6, m1, k1. 20 sts.

Round 3 K1, m1, k8, m1, k2, m1, k8, m1, k1. 24 sts.

Round 4 K

Round 5 K10, m1, k4, m1, k10. 26 sts.

Round 6-7 (2 rnds) K

Round 8 K11, m1, k4, m1, k11. 28 sts.

Round 9-10 (2 rnds) K

Round 11 K2, m1, k2, m1, k8, m1, k4, m1, k8, m1, k2, m1, k2. 34 sts.

Round 12 K

Round 13 Start short row for shaping forehead:

K3, w&t, p6, w&t, k7, w&t, p8, w&t, (k2, m1, k4, m1, k3), w&t, p12, w&t, k13, w&t, p14, w&t, (k5, m1, k4, m1, k to end). 38 sts.
Round 14 K

Round 15 Start short row for shaping head (two sequences of short rows):

I. K5, w&t, p10, w&t, k11, w&t, p12, w&t, (k3, m1, k6, m1, k4), w&t, p16, w&t, k17, w&t, p18, w&t, (k6, m1, k6, m1, k7), w&t, p22, w&t,

II. k15, w&t, p8, w&t, k9, w&t, p10, w&t, k11, w&t, p12, w&t, k13, w&t, p14, w&t, k15, w&t, p16, w&t, k17, w&t, p18, w&t, k to end. 42 sts.

Round 16-17 (2 rnds) K

(neck)

Round 18 K18, k2tog, k2, ssk, k18. 40 sts.

Round 19, 21, 23, 25 K

Round 20 K18, k2tog, ssk, k18. 38 sts.

Round 22 K4, m1, k30, m1, k4. 40 sts.

Round 24 K5, m1, k30, m1, k5. 42 sts.

Round 26 Start short row shaping for chest:

K40, w&t, p38, w&t, k37, w&t, p36, w&t, k35, w&t, p34, w&t, k33, w&t, p32, w&t, k31, w&t, p30, w&t, (k10, m1, k10, m1, k9), w&t, p30, w&t, k29, w&t, p28, w&t, (k9, m1, k10, m1, k8), w&t, p28, w&t, k27, w&t, p26, w&t, (k8, m1, k10, m1, k7), w&t, p26, w&t, k25, w&t, p24, w&t, k to end. 48 sts.

(body)

Round 27-46 (20rnds) K

Start to fill the doll with stuffing to desired firmness. Do not overstuff. Continue filling as you go.

Round 47 K17, ssk, k10, k2tog, k17. 46 sts.

Round 48-49 (2 rnds) K

Round 50 K16, ssk, k10, k2tog, k16. 44 sts.

Round 51-52 (2 rnds) K

Round 53 K12, m1, k5, m1, k10, m1, k5, m1, k12. 48 sts.

Round 54-55 (2 rnds) K

Round 56 K12, m1, k7, m1, k10, m1, k7, m1, k12. 52 sts.

Round 57-58 (2 rnds) K

Round 59 K20, k2tog 3 times, ssk 3 times, k20. 46 sts.

R60-61 (2 rnds) K

R62 K17, k2tog 3 times, ssk 3 times, k17. 40 sts.

R63-64 (2 rnds) K

R65 K14, k2tog 3 times, ssk 3 times, k14. 34 sts.

R66-67 (2 rnds) K

(start closing)

R68 K3, k2tog, (k2, k2tog) 3 times, (ssk, k2) 3 times, ssk, k3. 26 sts.

R69 K

R70 K2, k2tog, (k1, k2tog) 3 times, (ssk, k1) 3 times, ssk, k2. 18 sts.

R71 K

R72 K, k2tog 4 times, ssk 4 times, k. 10 sts

Break yarn. Using tapestry needle, thread yarn tail through all 10 stitches. Pull tightly to close.

Front Leg (make 2)

Make long-tail cast on 18 sts, leaving tail enough to sew the leg to the body later. Place marker, join to knit in the round, careful not to twist.

R1 K11, w&t, p4, w&t, k5, w&t, p6, w&t, k to end. 18 sts.

R2-5 (4 rnds) K

R6 K6, k2tog, k2, ssk, k6. 16 sts.

R7-10 (4 rnds) K

R11 K5, k2tog, k2, ssk, k5. 14 sts.

R12-15 (4 rnds) K

R16 K4, k2tog, k2, ssk, k4. 12 sts.

17 Remove marker, k6, place marker. Set as the beginning of a new round.

R18 K7, w&t, p2, w&t, k3, w&t, p4, w&t, k5, w&t, p6, w&t, (k1, m1, k4, m1, k2), w&t, p10, w&t, k12. 14 sts.

R19 K4, m1, k6, m1, k4. 16 sts.

R20 K

R21 K1, ssk, k2, k2tog, k2, ssk, k2, k2tog, k1. 12 sts.

R22 K1, k2tog, k1, ssk, k2tog, k1, ssk, k1. 8 sts.

Break yarn. Using tapestry needle, thread yarn tail through all 8 stitches. Pull tightly to close.

Back Leg (make 2)

Make long-tail cast on 20 sts, leaving tail enough to sew the leg to the body later. Place marker, join to knit in the round, careful not to twist.

R1 K12, w&t, p4, w&t, k5, w&t, p6, w&t, k7, w&t, p8, w&t, k to end. 20 sts.

R2-3 (2 rnds) K

R4 K7, k2tog, k2, ssk, k7. 18 sts.

R5-6 (2 rnds) K

R7 K6, k2tog, k2, ssk, k6. 16 sts.

R8-9 (2 rnds) K

R10 K5, k2tog, k2, ssk, k5. 14 sts.

R11 Remove marker, k7, place marker. Set as the beginning of a new round.

R12 K8, w&t, p2, w&t, k to end.

R13 K2tog, k10, ssk. 12 sts.

R14-18 (5 rnds) K

R18 K7, w&t, p2, w&t, k3, w&t, p4, w&t, k5, w&t, p6, w&t, (k1, m1, k4, m1, k2), w&t, p10, w&t, k12. 14 sts.

R19 K4, m1, k6, m1, k4. 16 sts.

R21 K1, ssk, k2, k2tog, k2, ssk, k2, k2tog, k1. 12 sts.

R22 K1, k2tog, k1, ssk, k2tog, k1, ssk, k1. 8 sts.

Break yarn. Using tapestry needle, thread yarn tail through all 8 stitches. Pull tightly to close.

Ears (make 2)

The ears are knitted flat in garter stitch pattern.

With #7 needles, long-tail CO 17 sts, leaving tail enough to sew the leg to the body later.

Row #

1 K6, ssk, k1, k2tog, k6. 15 sts.

2 and every

even row K

3 K5, ssk, k1, k2tog, k5. 13 sts.

5 K4, ssk, k1, k2tog, k4. 11 sts.

7 K1, ssk, k5, k2tog, k1. 9 sts

9 K

11 K1, ssk, k3, k2tog, k1. 7 sts

13 K

15 K1, ssk, k1, k2tog, k1. 5 sts

17 K

19 K1, sk2p, k1. 3 sts

Break yarn. Using tapestry needle, thread yarn tail through all 3 stitches. Pull tightly to close. Weave the yarn tail through the edge.

Tail

Make long-tail cast on 15 sts, leaving tail enough to sew the leg to the body later. Place marker, join to knit in the round, careful not to twist.

Round #

1-10 (10 rnds) K

11 K13, w&t, p11, w&t, k to end.

12 K

13 K2tog, k to end. 14 sts.

14 K

15 K12, ssk. 13 sts.

16-17 (2 rnds) K

18 K11, w&t, p9, w&t, k to end.

19 K

20 K2tog, k to end. 12 sts.

21 K

22 K10, ssk. 11 sts.

23 K

24 K2tog, k7, ssk. 9 sts.

25 K

26 K2tog, k5, ssk. 7 sts.

27 K

28 K2tog, k3, ssk. 5 sts.

Break yarn. Using tapestry needle, thread yarn tail through all 5 stitches. Pull tightly to close.

Finishing

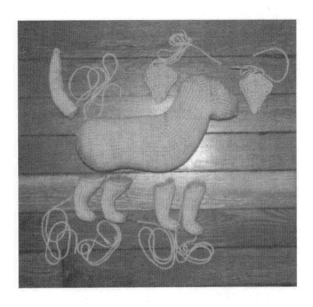

Stuff the legs and tail, then sew in their places.

Sew the ears in their places.

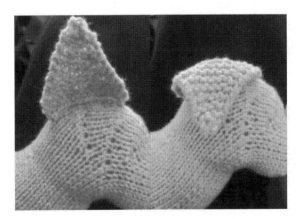

Sew the eyes and nose.

Printed in Great Britain
by Amazon

30202635R00051